99p
17,33

VICT(
CORI

C000260939

S. Daniell

Tor Mark Press · Penryn

The photographs
The aim of this book is to show life in nineteenth century Cornwall but life did not change dramatically at the turn of the century, and several fine photographers then began to record the old way of life, so we have included a few photographs which are not strictly 'Victorian'.

Title page photograph: A tinner's home, work and family, with New Wendron Consols ('Poldark Mine') in the background, probably about 1860

Second edition first published 1989 by
Tor Mark Press, Islington Wharf,
Penryn, Cornwall TR10 8AT
Formerly published under the title *Old Cornwall*

© 1989 Tor Mark Press

ISBN 0-85025-315-2

Acknowledgements
The publishers are grateful to the Cornwall Local Studies Library, Redruth for permission to reproduce the lower photograph on page 15 and to the Royal Institution of Cornwall for all the other photographs; they are also grateful to the Curator of the Royal Institution, Roger Penhallurick, for his help with picture research.

Printed in Great Britain by Century Litho (Truro) Ltd, Falmouth.

I

THE CORNISH AT WORK

IT IS NOT SURPRISING, IN A COUNTY WITH SUCH A LONG AND indented coastline as Cornwall, that fishing should have played a major part in its economy. Lobsters and crabs were caught along the rocky coast; cod, conger, ling, hake and bream offshore by hook and line; and oysters were reared in enormous quantities in the creeks of the Fal, as well as in the Helford River. More important were the mackerel and herring fisheries of the Spring and late Autumn but the principal catch in former centuries was without doubt the pilchard. This arrived in vast shoals about harvest time, when the 'corn was in the shock', as the Cornish would say. First appearing off Wolf Rock, the fish made their way up either coast from Land's End. Thus the busiest fishing ports were those in the extreme south-west—Sennen, St. Ives, Mousehole and Newlyn, for instance—although almost every cove had its own seine or fishing company.

This usually comprised three boats, a fishing fleet in miniature, which in the richest areas had allocated to it a particular stretch of coast called a stem, marked out by poles on the shore. As the value of the stems as fishing grounds varied considerably, their allocation at the beginning of each season was determined by boat races or the drawing of lots. Sometimes it was necessary for two or more seines to share, fishing at different times.

Seines were given individual names—the Trusty, Unity, Prosperous, Olive Branch and Diamond seines operated out of St. Mawes, for instance, and from Mevagissey the Concord, Dolphin, Favourite, Venus and Cordelia—but individually the boats were named according to their functions. The seine boat, broad, low and sharp, and rowed by six men, carried the principal net, which weighed some three tons and was a quarter of a mile in length. Behind came the follower, or volyer, a craft of similar appearance but carrying a smaller net, called the tuck. A lesser boat, known as the lurker, brought up the rear; on board was the master seiner, and from this boat the various operations were co-ordinated. In the west of the county particularly, where the strength of the tides kept boats well inshore, directions were often given by a man stationed on a vantage point ashore. Called the huer or balker, he was provided with a tiny watch-house to protect him from all weathers, since he was at his station many days before the shoals arrived, as were the seines along the shore below. Huers' huts still remain to be seen at Newquay and St. Ives. When the balker sighted the red-brown flurry in the water which marked an approaching shoal he picked up the five foot long speaking trumpet with which he was equipped and through this bellowed to the boats waiting at anchor below 'Hevva, hevva!', meaning 'A shoal, a shoal!'. Thereafter, he controlled the movements of the boats by means of white 'flags' called bushes, one of which was held in each hand. These were made of white cloth stretched over bent canes on the end of a stick, although furze branches were also used occasionally, sometimes even the huer's hat. As quickly as possible the boats obeyed his instructions which drew them nearer to the shoal, and the order 'Shoot the seine'—that is 'Drop the net'—was bawled out at the exact moment through the trumpet. Thereupon, the seine boat rapidly encircled the fish, drawing with it the curtain-like seine net, held tight between cork and sinker. Then quickly the final gap was closed by the little stop net and the whole, containing perhaps 3,000,000 fish, if the shoal was a large one, was drawn closer inshore by capstans on the beach and moored all round by grapples.

On shore, in a state of great excitement, the whole village would be waiting, eagerly anticipating several hard weeks' work—if the season's catches were good—preserving the fish for later consumption. Among the crowd were sure to be found a number of 'jousters', wives of fishermen who went round the countryside hawking pilchards. These were carried in baskets resting upon their backs and suspended by bands around their foreheads. The Newlyn fishwives were particularly well known for their black beaver hats and bright red cloaks. While all waited, the tuck net was lowered inside the seine net, and slowly raised to the surface when full, bringing with it each time a seething mass of leaping, silvery fish. Rapidly each load was transferred to the boats and thence to 'tuck baskets' to be carried away to the individual fish cellars beneath the houses or to the larger 'palaces', where the work was done around a central courtyard. Here the pilchards were laid in layers, with salt between, the workers having to keep pace with the overwhelming supply brought up from the beach, although tucking might be aban-

4

A group of 'jousters' — fishermen's wives who hawked pilchards in the countryside — seen here at Newlyn

Tucking pilchards off St Ives, about 1900

Roberts' Boatyard, Mevagissey

doned for a time if need be. The fear of fish dying while in the seine net kept all hands working at top speed, however. After landing, the fish were left in salt for about five weeks, being then washed and packed in casks, or hogsheads, weighted with large stones to press out the oil. This was the case with most of the fish, which was destined for the Roman Catholic countries of the Mediterranean for consumption during Lent. That which provided the winter diet of the Cornish themselves was treated in the same way, but any intended for the West Indies' slave population were twice cured on account of the tropic heat. The spent salt was thereafter sold to local farmers at about sixpence a bushel, and together with any waste fish, found its way on to the fields as a form of manure. The coarse oil, which streamed out through the staves to be collected in pits, was barrelled and sold, chiefly to the Royal Navy but also to foreign merchants and to 'soap boilers'. It is often said that Cornish women of those days had beautiful skins and hair on account of the Vitamin D in the fish that they handled, b ut at the same time there is no doubt that they, and everyone else involved, smelled strongly of pilchard: certainly most contemporary accounts of Cornwall make reference to the appalling stench of fish in coastal villages, the cobbled streets of which streamed with effluvia from the cellars—in one case straight into the local well.

The cost of a seine, together with all its equipment, including fish salt and barrels, ran into many hundreds of pounds, so that usually several men held shares and the profits of each catch were divided among them. To some extent this afforded protection against the vagaries of the pilchard which was their mainstay. In the 1830's, for instance, it virtually made no appearance for several seasons in succession, and the poor were brought to the brink of starvation; in 1871, on the other hand, nearly 46,000 hogsheads were exported, the record of the century. By this date, however, the seine fishing industry was in decline generally, the pilchard for some strange reason having deserted inshore waters. In the same way it was found that mackerel also were gradually leaving coastal waters and for a period these, as well as herring and pilchard, were caught farther from the shore by drifters. The two former were also salted and barrelled for export to Mediterranean countries, especially Italy, and Cornish ships sailed regularly to ports such as Leghorn, Naples and Venice.

The technique of drift fishing differed from seining, for the nets—

perhaps thirty or so fastened together—trailed out behind the boat, hanging like a great curtain in the deeper water. Fish which moved in with the tide then became entangled in the mesh. For many years these driving boats, as they were called, had been a source of irritation to inshore fishermen because of their continual trespass within the one and a half league limit set upon their activities, but initially the boats at least were Cornish and feelings did not run too high. When the railway came to Cornwall in 1859, however, a demand grew up in London for fresh fish from Cornwall, mackerel in particular, and competition for this increasing trade became fierce. A large number of East coast drifters and trawlers, from Lowestoft, Yarmouth and other ports, were by this time starting to fish off the south-west and the resentment they caused was increased by the fact that their crews practised Sunday fishing, an outrage to the devout Cornish, who never put to sea on the Sabbath. Towards the end of the century large up-country steam drifters were becoming common in Cornish waters, vessels more seaworthy and better equipped than local craft, with the result that the West Country fishing industry declined yet further. Dozens of seine and other fishing boats lay rotting in the coves of west Cornwall or were sold for other purposes. Thousands of men, formerly working at high pressure throughout the season, perhaps being at sea for as much as a week at a time, were thrown idle, their families hungry. Ancillary industries suffered too. Cooperages, bark houses, rope manufactories, sail lofts, boat building yards fell one after another into disuse. It was a blessing that with the coming of the railway after mid century, bringing with it an increasing number of holidaymakers, the fishing villages found another reason for their existence in the tourist trade.

Until the nineteenth century there is little doubt that the Cornish supplemented meagre wages and a near starvation diet by the barbarous practice of wrecking. Inshore piracy had been common enough in former centuries and it was but a small step from the plundering of a vessel at sea to the pillage of one driven ashore in storm. The Crown in fact had sole claim to any ship wrecked along the Cornish coast but many wealthy landowners whose estates bordered the sea declared this privilege to be their own, and grew richer from the spoils taken by force of arms from helpless ships and their crews. Not unnaturally their example was followed by the poor, who at least had some excuse in their lack of decent food, clothing and shelter. The news of an impending wreck having spread throughout the countryside, literally thousands would gather on the cliffs to watch and follow for miles the hapless vessel as it drifted before the storm on to the rocks. Particularly notorious were the mobs of violent tinners who gathered like vultures for the Mount's Bay wrecks and there is little doubt that occasional atrocities were committed. Armed with hatchets, ropes and crowbars, and in a fever of excitement, the wreckers were more than the military or excise men could cope with, let alone exhausted sailors. Fever became frenzy when casks of brandy came ashore and were broken open there and then; those who opposed the drunken and hungry tinner under such circumstances could expect little mercy. Not that he alone engaged in this miserable business, for men, women and children from the farms and fishing villages, as well as the occasional customs officer, mayor or clergyman, gathered in their hundreds to pick any ship clean. With luck, the broken vessel might contain bullion, jewels and plate; almost as welcome, because more easily put to good use, were such luxuries as tea, tobacco, and bales of cotton or silk. More common, however, were Continental wines, brandies and liqueurs, but all was welcome and rapidly carried off 'by the country' on ponies, carts or willing shoulders. The rigging, sails and timbers of a vessel usually met the same fate within a matter of hours, while even the few pitiful possessions of the drowning and dying sailors were hastily snatched and divided.

Whether more culpable forms of wrecking existed in former times in Cornwall it is hard to say. The temptation was undoubtedly there to lure a vessel inshore into dangerous waters by showing misleading lights along the cliffs but there are no cases on record of anyone caught and punished for such a barbarous act. On the other hand, it is said that the lighthouse on Scilly failed to shine for no good reason now and again. On some stretches of Cornwall's coasts, wrecks and strandings were so frequent each winter that there was hardly the need to add to their number by luring further vessels ashore. In any southerly storm around west Cornwall, for example, a dozen ships might come ashore in the coves or on the beaches from Land's End to the Lizard.

Wrecking died a natural death during the first half of the nineteenth century, partly from an increase in the forces of law and order and partly from the expansion in the coastguard service in the 1830's, when it was put under Admiralty control. Close watch on the coast in bad weather after this date enabled the authorities to prepare for a wreck, and thus for any possible wreckers. The expansion also of the excise to put down smuggling, the rise of the lifeboat service and the provision of lighthouses along the coast, also contributed to the demise of the old-time wrecker.

Another and more harmless source of luxuries than wrecking, especially in the Scilly Isles, was smuggling. This too, was more rife in the early days of the nineteenth century, until such time as the surveillance of the coast by preventive boats and revenue cutters was increased about 1820. Even then, the wild coast of cliffs and coves, the endless hideouts in the form of sea-caves or winding wooded creeks, made the work of the 'moonshine brigade' relatively easy. Added to this was the fact that, as with wrecking, few Cornish were uninvolved and even fewer were informers. Most smuggling gangs were highly organised, with armed men who drove off—and if necessary murdered—those who tried to interfere, and with watchers placed on the heights to light beacons if danger threatened in the form of the excise men. Cornish craft, often built specially for the purpose, plied back and forth across the Channel, carrying tobacco, silks and laces, tea, and most often, brandy, Geneva and rum. Chiefly they came from Roscoff, in Brittany, or from Guernsey. On moonless nights, sometimes even by day, the contraband was brought ashore, where hundreds of ponies waited. In some cases these were specially trained, fierce kickers, well greased, manes and tails clipped, so that they could not be caught in the event of trouble. As often as not the preventive man kept clear, and the preventive boats too, since it was not unknown for the one to be shot and the other sunk or captured, despite the prospect of transportation or the terrors of Bodmin gaol for the guilty. After mid century, a Cornish boat caught in the hands of 'fair traders' was sawn in three parts as punishment, so that French craft were chartered instead, these dropping the contraband overboard to anchor off shore, to be picked up later. Once on the beach, the illicit goods disappeared like magic, hidden in cave and mine adit in the cliffs, or taken to the country to find their way into hedge or hayrick, cottage hideaway, sickbed, coffin or even voluminous skirt, as the urgency of the moment demanded.

Whilst longshore life in Cornwall traditionally revolved around the harvests of the sea, illicit or otherwise, those farther removed from the coast depended principally upon mining or farming for their livelihood. At the beginning of the nineteenth century much of the inland part of the county was uncultivated moorland and waste. Farming occurred chiefly along the coast and extended only a little way inland, chiefly following the valleys, so that only about one third of the county was cultivated. An equal amount was under furze and ploughed over only rarely, to be cropped two or three times and then abandoned in a fashion akin to primitive shifting agriculture. One reason for this was that by using this method, the farmer avoided the payment of tithes. The remainder was unenclosed moorland and tor, high and boulder strewn. Excepting the mining districts, therefore, all which was not farmland was virtually uninhabited at that date.

The typical Cornish farm of the last century was small, sufficiently so in most cases to be entirely a family concern. There might also be pauper children employed, since they were always apprenticed to farming by the parish overseers, but the number of wage-earning labourers was not large. Then, as now, the fields were small, perhaps about three acres on average, and protected by Cornish hedges of stone. Soils too, have not changed. Large areas were blanketed by a gravelly 'growan' derived from the underlying granite, an acid soil supporting bracken and heather. There were also large tracts of peat bog over which rights of turbary were exercised and the peat cut for winter fuel, as in Ireland today. On the higher granite moors, May month saw the arrival of large flocks and herds. They were gathered by herdsmen over wide areas of the surrounding lowlands for this 'summering' and departed with the autumn rains: native black cattle, small and hardy; gaunt and graceless workhorses; and smaller numbers of sheep, coarse-woolled and half wild creatures, ill suited to the conditions on the moors. Many indeed were lost due to lack of food and shelter in the wet season because, according to a contemporary account, from 'custom, indulgence or preferring the risk', the Cornish farmer never took the necessary precautions. As it was common pasture, the animals roamed freely, each with its identifying mark, grazing among the countless pools and rivulets caused by the burrowings of stream tinners. On these waters the latter reared thousands of geese for market; rustling of stock frequently took place but can hardly have been easy, even at dead of night.

The lowland farms of Cornwall were chiefly on slaty soils, although there were exceptions, good and bad. The schist soils around St. Keverne, for instance, are remarkably fertile and in the nineteenth century provided much of the grain for the mining population to the north; by contrast, the adjacent soils derived from serpentine rock which cover nearly all the remainder of the Lizard are notoriously barren and then supported only sturdy 'goonhillies' (ponies) and wild cattle amid the gorse and heath. As for the farms on killas, or clay-slate, their owners had to contend with iron hard soil in summer and with waterlogged fields and lanes in winter. So impassable did the latter become that fines were imposed on farmers allowing them to get overgrown, for this hindered their drying out. A further nuisance throughout much of the county was the stony nature of the ground, particularly the presence of vast amounts of white quartz or 'spar'. As much as possible was incorporated into the hedges and as late as 1900 children were employed during school holidays picking stone at 6d a day.

All Cornish soils were sour and acid—as they are today—and benefited greatly from the application of sand, either the salt sand from below high water mark or limy shell sand from the dunes. Farms near the coast were most fortunate in this respect, being able regularly to send carts down the 'sanding roads', as the tracks to the sea were called. In the early days those inland were reached as far as possible by river barge, and thence by pack mule or cart. Most of Cornwall's rivers have silted badly in the last hundred years and formerly sand barges went regularly well upstream, to Tresillian for example, carrying Falmouth harbour sand. This was most highly prized of all and was dredged up off St. Mawes, but as a source of 'manure' it was spoiled in the nineteenth century when waste from the copper mines of Gwennap permeated some of the creeks of the Fal. Sea sand for farms was also obtained in great quantities from Gunwalloe, Perranporth, the Camel estuary, Trebarwith and Bude, as well as the beaches along Gerrans Bay and St. Austell Bay on the south coast. The Camel sand went inland by rail and even traction engine, while the Bude canal was built partly to deal with such traffic. A railway was suggested from Perranporth to Truro in the 1830's for much the same purpose.

On the southern estuaries, as well as that of the Camel, barges also worked back and forth with 'ore-weed', that is sea-weed, which when spread on the fields not only acted as a valuable manure but to some extent compensated for the serious mineral deficiencies of the soil caused by the torrential rains of winter. In particular it was applied to the potato crop, which tasted accordingly. Other manures used were lime, from Devon limestone burned in scores of kilns along the Cornish coast; South American and African guanos (sea-bird excrement imported in bulk); plus waste fish and salt from the pilchard industry. During the Napoleonic wars, when the European pilchard markets were closed to Cornwall, large quantities of fish were available as cheap manure and it even became the practice for farmers to own seines and so obtain unlimited supplies with which to add fertility to their soils.

In the old days the usual crops in Cornwall were wheat, barley and oats, together with grass for winter feed as hay. With the relatively crude farm implements then in use, a man could be expected to plough an acre in one day. For this he was paid four or five shillings, but for this thirsty work was given also a daily gallon of beer, which cost about half as much again. Oxen were principally used for ploughing—even as late as 1900 on one Cornish farm. Although extremely slow, they were cheaper to keep than a horse and required far less attention. Moreover, when the time came, they provided a few hundredweight of welcome beef. Usually they were fed on wheat straw instead of hay in winter, although much of the former was sold in some parishes to shipwrights for burning beneath their boats when caulking.

Much the same wages were earned at reaping and mowing time in the early days of the century. During the weeks when the crops were gathered in it was customary for hundreds of miners and fishermen to make their way into the fields after their usual spell of work, and labour there until after sundown. The womenfolk, who like their husbands, were muscular, weatherbeaten and usually old before their time from drudgery and privation, also assisted. Helping too were their children, most of whom left school at an early age, if indeed they attended one at all. Reaping was done in the age-old fashion with sickle or scythe by men or women working in rhythmic lines across the fields, while other workers followed deftly binding the grain into sheaves. These were then set up in 'shocks' upon the stubble or 'arrish', awaiting removal to the rickyard. In the west of the county until quite recently it was the general practice to leave the sheaves stacked in the fields in groups of about two hundred, each group forming a round 'arrish mow', a feature peculiar to Cornwall. In earlier days each mow could be threshed with flails by two men in a day; thereafter the grain was sold, each buyer taking his grain to a miller, who usually received as toll one twelfth of the total quantity ground. The resulting wheat bran was used for feeding poultry. The straw was gathered in for winter feed; wheat straw for oxen, that from oats and barley for cattle. The hay crop was reserved for horses, although it must be remembered that many farmers made use of mules bred outside the county, as well as donkeys, Goss Moor ponies and the hardy little goonhillies. Finally, when all was gathered in, the poorest of the poor exercised their time honoured right to glean the harvest fields.

During the wars with France in the early nineteenth century, England's trade with Europe was almost at a standstill, so that Continental corn did not enter English ports. After the wars, the introduction of the Corn Laws in England had a similar effect and little grain was imported into the country on account of the high duties imposed. Thus corn was scarce and dear in Cornwall, as elsewhere, with the result that the poor suffered intensely. During these years rioting mobs on the brink of starvation were common in parts of the county; frequently they tried to prevent the loading of ships with corn destined for up-country markets, where it fetched a high price. To offset this shortage of grain more land was brought under the plough to grow potatoes some of which, together with skimmed milk, were fed to the many pigs which were reared—if reared be the right term, since they were permitted to wander at will scavenging in gardens, allotments and fields. The nuisance they created, rooting up the ground, breaking hedges and making filth generally was all too well known in earlier days. Nevertheless, they contributed important items to the Cornishman's diet and in periods of potato shortage—slow farming methods and lack of mechanisation often meant that the crop was still in the ground when the first frosts came—elm leaves were assiduously gathered and boiled to feed them. At the appropriate time it was customary for all the pigs in a limited area to be slaughtered on the same day, on which occasion all hands turned out to assist. Each carcase was scalded, and then salted in brine contained in vast tubs or slate troughs in the salting room of the farmhouse.

During the second half of the century the nature of Cornish farming began to change. It was discovered, for instance, that improved types of

A farmyard near Blackwater, about 1890

A blacksmith and his apprentice shoeing a horse, St Agnes, 1900

Threshing by steam at Trewhella Farm, St Hillary

The growing of early Spring flowers became a mainstay of the Isles of Scilly in the late nineteenth century; here narcissi are being bunched for packing and despatch

wheat being introduced in England did not grow well in Cornwall with its frequent rains, and as a result pastoral farming became increasingly widespread. But the principal change came with the building of the Cornwall Railway in 1859. There was already a network of subsidiary lines built during the railway mania of the hungry 30's and 40's, as well as a number of better roads, and these now acted as feeders for the new main line to London and Covent Garden. All those parts of Cornwall suited to the growing of early vegetables, such as the Mount's Bay area, and the sunny slopes around the Fal estuary, found themselves with a growing market to supply in the metropolis. In the early 1880's, moreover, the first box of cut spring flowers—a hat-box, it is said—was sent from the Isles of Scilly to Covent Garden as an experiment, and proved so profitable on sale that flower growing in the islands increased rapidly thereafter. By the turn of the century over 500 tons of flowers were being produced annually and thousands of boxes of these fragile blooms, along with crates of broccoli and sacks of potatoes bound for Covent Garden, as well as mackerel destined for Billingsgate, found their way to London on the swift trains which ran daily from Penzance.

Though fishing and farming were staple industries of Cornwall in the nineteenth century, mining was the industry which provided the economic mainstay of the county. Something like one person in four in West Cornwall was dependent upon mining and its ancillary industries. These were particularly numerous and involved many trades: tallow chandlers; ropemakers; carters and mule drivers; ore samplers and foundry hands; gunpowder manufacturers; masons, bricklayers and carpenters. For every hundred directly employed on or in a mine, there were something like six hundred who indirectly found employment. Nearby farmers pastured horses or pack animals; shipping places near at hand employed men on the inward or outward trade in ore, coal and mine timbers; local innkeepers and shopkeepers prospered on the spending of miners' pay. Thus mining was the great mainstay of the county except perhaps in the agricultural parishes north of the Camel.

Miners fell into two categories, known as tributers and tutworkers. The former were more highly skilled and carried out work on a contract basis, in gangs known as 'pares', paying a 'tribute' proportion to the mine owners of the value of the ore they won. Tutworkers did the more humdrum work driving levels and sinking shafts, paid at so much per fathom. Other underground workers who might loosely be classed as miners were timbermen, who were responsible for the safe support of the workings, and pitmen who tended the pumping machinery within the mine. Supervising them all were the captains, men who were the equivalent of managers. A big mine might have five or six, in charge of various operations during the different cores of the day or night. These captains came up from the ranks of working miners; largely self-taught practical men with little or no formal education and in some cases even unable to read.

Boys were employed underground, and before official regulations were brought in during the 1870's, they were often put to work there well below the age of ten, even in mines far deeper than collieries. Girls or women, however, have never found work below surface, although used in large numbers in the dressing or preparation of ore once it had been hauled out of the mine. Most miners were young, for it was not a calling for an old man or one who was not agile. Three cores or shifts were worked in all big mines, though shorter periods than eight hours were sometimes worked in hot or badly ventilated mines. The work was hard, particularly so in the days before the 1870's when rock drills were introduced. All holes had to be bored by hand ready for blasting with gunpowder, and the orestuff then barrowed back to the nearest shaft where it could be hauled to surface. This was in roughly hewn small levels, inadequately ventilated and lit, in which the temperature was enough to make every man perspire the whole core through. This period of eight hours' work was too much in deep mines that were particularly hot and there six hours was all that a man could manage. It must be remembered that before his core and, even worse, after it, a miner had to reach his allotted piece of work (his 'pitch') by ladders. The climb out of a mine, up a long succession of perhaps thirty ladders, hand over hand and rung after rung for a thousand feet of near vertical climb was nothing short of punishment. This, after all, is the height of a mountain in Britain, and 1,000 feet was not regarded as deep by the standards of Cornwall's mines. Young miners are said to have raced each other up the ladderways but older miners struggled up, their hearts and lungs taxed to the uttermost. In time they could only manage to go down to the shallow levels, and after this quit the mine.

Heart disease was commonplace and 'falling away' from the ladders, due to an uncontrollable spell of sudden dizziness, was the cause of innumerable deaths over the years. Ailments of the chest were no less frequent, brought on by years of work in an atmosphere which would have been considered unbearable by anyone not brought up to it from childhood. Deep underground, the 'fug' caused by the burning of innumerable tallow candles, the presence of a mass of sweating humanity, exploding gunpowder and decaying timber—plus a lack of all sanitary facilities—all in a humid atmosphere, defies description. Such conditions, of course, are very different from the present day, for mining has been transformed in the past century.

Among the various other mishaps in which miners were all too often involved, blasting accidents were usually the most tragic. These personal disasters maimed and often blinded a man, rendering him unable to work and support those dependent upon him. They were caused either by accidental sparks from the iron bar used for tamping in the charge, or when a hole misfired as a result perhaps of a poorly made rush-fuse. Having crept forward fearfully to see what had gone wrong when this happened, a miner might be peering at the hole or starting gingerly to clear it when it exploded inches from his face. . . .

When one considers the conditions under which the nineteenth century miner laboured, one might expect him to have enjoyed more than a living wage. Yet this was far from the case, most miners earning at best twelve or fifteen shillings a week on average. Tributers did better than this—sometimes: at others they might fare much worse. A lot depended on their luck as well as their skill, and without luck they might work for a month for less than a pound. In most mines the 'bargains' or contracts made by the tributers lasted for two months. Paydays were thus a long way apart and to tide the men over an advance in the form of 'subsist' was made by the mine company. If this was insufficient—for with only poor 'gettings' mounting up slowly, subsist was not automatic—men relied to a large extent upon 'tick' with the local shopkeeper. This might continue for months until such time as a lucky 'bargain' enabled them to break out of debt. There was the occasional rich strike when a pare of tributers might share fifty or even a hundred pounds between them on payday, but this was rare. The average family had, of course, three or four wage earners in it, for the children were put to work just as soon as this was physically possible. There was employment at surface aplenty on the mines, tending stamps, the buddles or other tin dressing machinery, or for the

sturdier children picking, cobbing and sorting ore on the mines pro-
ducing copper. Although wages for this might be 3d, 4d, or at most 5d
a day, it was still a valuable addition to a family income. The majority
of married miners also cultivated a small plot of ground around or near
their cottages and there they grew food to supplement what could be
bought with their wages. In this way, many miners were also small-
holders, though not, one suspects, from choice. After a long core in the
depths of a mine, breaking into cultivation a rocky parcel of moorland
was only done from necessity. Potatoes formed the main crop, as this
gave the heaviest yield yard for yard and could be stored to last through
the winter. As in contemporary Ireland, the humble 'potatoe' was all
important in Cornwall's domestic economy. Potatoes, too, or at least
the waste ones which grew rotten and unfit to eat, could be fed to the
pig which most families reared.

Tinners, the first workers employed in searching and digging for the
metal at surface prior to the advent of true mining, were traditionally
regarded as a rough and riotous class, given to wandering and living on
some of the moorland streamworks like semi-vagrants. This changed
somewhat with the development of mines and more permanent mining
districts. Mining villages sprang up, such as Carharrack and Lanner
in the important copper mining parish of Gwennap. Later in the
century in east Cornwall hamlets such as Pensilva and Upton Cross
burgeoned with the rise of mining around Caradon. This nineteenth
century generation of miners were less prone to riot than their forebears, perhaps, although there are several accounts of uprisings in the
hungry 1840's. But they were still a rough lot, hard drinking, coarse and
addicted to such brutal pastimes as stoning matches between the mines
of rival villages. There is one account of a group of miners marching
from St. Day to Redruth for a mob fight: they met a dog en route and
we may judge their savage natures from the fact that they killed it and
stained the flag which they were carrying with its blood. It was, of
course, a brutal age, in Cornwall as elsewhere; colliers, navvies and
other labourers in counties up-country were no better. The romance of
most things historical tends to colour our regard for the past and in this
case the popular but in fact very mistaken image of the average Cornish
miner of a century ago is of a gentle family man, teetotal and an upright
'Methodee'. Wesley and his teachings had a marked effect upon the
rough nature of the tinners but the number of kiddleywinks (beer-

houses) and inns clustered around the old centres of mining far out-numbered the chapels and churches of any kind.

Living under conditions of squalor at home and worse than squalor at work, it is creditable to miners as a class that they were no worse than they were. In one respect they differed greatly from colliers, with whom a comparison might otherwise be drawn; they had no propensity for strikes and union action. A few strikes did take place but they were never well organised or long lasting and even after the end of the century, long after the unionisation of labour elsewhere in Britain, there was no such activity whatever in Cornish mining. The nature of the men's work, particularly under the system of tributing, which may be likened to a form of sub-contracting, did not lend itself to concerted action. The Cornish motto 'One and All' might signify solidarity but this was conspicuously absent whenever it was needed most.

The safety valve for the discontent that smouldered in the mining districts was emigration. Individual miners with more initiative and more foresight than their fellows were the first to go, some of them being truly pioneers in opening up new mining fields on other con-tinents. In Californian and Australian gold rushes Cornish miners were numbered but it was more to the copper districts of South Australia and Michigan and the lead district of Illinois that they went. But Cornish miners were to be found literally all over the world, from Chile to Newfoundland, Cuba to India. The gradual exhaustion of Cornwall's home mines drove these Cousin Jacks everywhere across the earth, culminating in a massive wave of emigration to the newly developed gold mines of the Rand in the 1880's and 1890's when Cornish mining passed into a swift decline. By 1900 there was only a handful of tin mines surviving, with less than a twentieth of the number of men working underground that had been half a century before.

The decline in Cornwall's staple industry, mining, coincided to some degree with the rise in production of another mineral, china-clay. For this as much as for tin, Cornwall has since become world renowned. China-clay is formed by the decomposition of granite, and in a pure state is found in very few places in the world, as for instance in China, where 'kaolin' was worked over a thousand years ago. The deposits in Cornwall were first exploited in the eighteenth century, by the Plymouth potter William Cookworthy, and thereafter by various Staffordshire potters, including such well known names as Wedgwood, Minton and Spode. Although initially discovered on Tregoning Hill near Porthleven, the principal area for the production of clay was on the granite hills to the north of St. Austell, on Hensbarrow. As was the case in the development of mines the first china-clay pits, of which only about seven existed in 1810, were small and worked in primitive fashion. They were, in fact, little more than shallow depressions in the ground perhaps about ten feet in depth and were abandoned when they became too deep to be baled out by bucket or by some form of crude hand pump. Even the largest of these 'works' employed only about a dozen or so hands, most of whom were men employed on the strenuous task of digging out the clay. Naturally this contained impurities such as pieces of rock and unwanted minerals, so that it was necessary to barrow it to the nearest water—often part of a stream which had been diverted to the clay-face—to wash out the heavier waste and retain the fine white kaolin. There was always much more of the former, chiefly quartz sand, than the latter, so that it had to be shovelled constantly and rapidly out of the pit and tipped on the surrounding moorland, again a man's job. Although free of sand the water, white as milk, still contained foreign matter, and to get rid of this the slurry was made to pass through a series of settling pits. These were usually attended by a boy, as their supervision was so uncomplicated. In the last pit the soft white china-clay, now reasonably pure, sank to the bottom and the water above it was drained off through a series of bung-holes. In this way the kaolin dried out to the consistency of thick cream, after which it was barrowed into shallower pans for further drying, by the action of sun and wind. This method of separating out fine and coarse materials was crude by today's standards, with the result that when clay in the pans was cut into blocks and lifted, the underside of each had to be scraped by hand to remove coarser material which had settled there. This task normally fell to the lot of women, since the work was clean and easy and, as most of the dozens of small pits which opened up after 1800 were family concerns, no doubt two or three brothers, their wives and children, often sufficed as the complete labour force for any one.

These people led entirely outdoor and healthy lives, free from industrial diseases, as well as the dangers and sorry conditions of work that the Cornish miner stoically accepted as his lot—no doubt the reason why the latter, when out of work, considered it beneath him to 'go clay'. Even so, for the menfolk in china-clay the work was undoubtedly heavy, excavating the soft granite or barrowing away many hundreds of cubic yards of wet sand or clay from dawn till dusk and, on occasion, even during the hours of darkness by the light of candles. There was little difference, in fact, from the healthy lives of farm labourers working in the fields about them, and their womenfolk, too, were fortunate by working standards of the day. Turned out in white aprons, bonnets and 'sleeves', they scraped the clay at tables set beneath little 'huts' of thatched hurdles, although one suspects that it was the dry clay rather than the brawny and healthy women that required protection from the next quick Cornish downpour.

Nearly all the clay from these early pits was casked, taken by cart to the St. Austell Bay ports of Charlestown, Pentewan and, later, Par to be shipped to the Potteries. Already, however, some was also being used by the paper and textile industries and this amount gradually increased, making it essential for the ever deepening clay pits to be worked and drained by machinery as time went by. By mid century in most concerns, raising clay slurry to surface as well as surplus water was effected by pump, usually powered by a waterwheel, while horses working whims helped to haul out the waste sand. Nevertheless, the labour force was still over 7,000. These people were employed on those tasks which no machine could then cope with: children on gathering moss for sealing the stone-walled drying pans; women on scraping clay; and men on such tasks as carting, the clearing of overburden, shovelling of sand, 'washing' at the clay face, supervising the pits and pans, by this time a more complex operation, and in some cases, making bricks and tiles from materials formerly regarded as waste.

Gradually during the second half of the century the old methods of air-drying were largely superseded by coal-fired kilns or 'drys', waterwheels by beam engines, 'washers' by power-hoses, horse and cart by mineral lines built into the china-clay country. In time, many of the pits, which by the 1890's numbered about one hundred and were in some cases hundreds of feet deep, began to obviate the need for rail transport by piping slurry direct to the drys on the quayside. Similarly, the whole process of clay production in the pit became increasingly mechanised to meet the growing demand for the product in paper making, textiles, pharmaceuticals, linoleum manufacture, the chemical and other industries.

II

THE CORNISH AT HOME

LIKE SO MANY FEATURES OF NINETEENTH CENTURY CORNWALL, the typical Cornish cottage which housed fisherman, farmworker, miner and quarryman alike, has virtually disappeared from the scene. Those that remain have been altered and extended almost beyond recognition, in order to bring them up to today's standards of accommodation and hygiene. In fact, to see cottages resembling those to be found in Cornwall one or two hundred years ago, and still unspoiled, it is necessary to go to the west of Ireland. There they abound, for progress has overtaken neither them nor their occupants, whose simple way of life also has much in common with the old-time Cornish.

Formerly thousands of these humble dwellings existed in Cornwall, particularly in the more populous mining districts. Characteristically they occurred not so much clustered in villages as scattered across the landscape in an apparently haphazard fashion. This random settlement was governed by the fact that the miner usually chose to rent a piece of waste ground which he could clear of bracken or gorse, hearten with sea-sand or other manure to grow a few crops, and build a cottage there into the bargain. The ground rent was low enough for the poorest man to find, but as part of the agreement the lease was drawn up on the three lives basis, whereby the house and the land, however much improved, reverted to the landowner on the death of the last of the three lives named in the lease as chosen by the tenant. Not infrequently, the arrangement lasted all too short a time, for death came earlier in those days and a man might find himself in danger of being dispossessed, unless able to pay the 'fine' customarily required to add new lives and so retain his lease of house and land.

Most cottages of this class were put together by their owner with the help of friends after their long day's work, so that generally they were of crude construction and met only the most basic requirements. It is said, however, that according to one custom, a man who erected a dwelling in a single night retained its freehold in perpetuity, so that all in all no great amount of time was spent in housebuilding. Of necessity

*Contrasts in entertainment: above, a garden party at Prideaux Place,
Padstow, in 1899 and below, a fair at Tolcarne, near Newquay, in 1886*

The Helston Furry Dance at Higher Pengwedna, 3 May 1904

The Padstow Obby-Oss in the 1920s

a minimum of cost, too, went into their construction. Four low walls sufficed, sometimes of granite boulders or rough slabs of clay-slate where these materials were readily available but more often of cob—a mixture of straw and the glutinous clay of which Cornwall has an excess. Sometimes the walls were made of sods of earth alone. The roof timbers as often as not were filched from a timely wreck, garnered from the nearest beach or brought home secretly from the mine. Upon them were laid either more sods or a thatch of straw, heather or reeds, the whole being secured against the wind by ropes and weights, as say, in Donegal today. More rarely, a cottage might have a roof of small slates rejected by a nearby quarry.

These primitive 'cabins', as they were usually called in their day, were excessively damp and dark within, moisture rising from the floor of beaten earth, seeping through the walls and all too often finding its way through a badly thatched roof. Such window openings as there might be were small and often had to await the finding of a piece or two of broken glass or a bottle end before completion. Nor was much comfort to be derived within from the crude and usually home made furniture— perhaps a hard wooden settle, a bench, and one or two stools, with a bed of sorts, usually of sacking stretched on a timber frame. Such luxuries as curtains, rugs, cushions and tablecloths were unheard of, as were ceilings or plastered walls. Inevitably there was no running water and for many cottages not even a convenient well, no sanitation and no form of illumination save the homemade rushlight, or a candle end brought home from the mine. Very soon a man and his wife would have a brood of children to fill their one-roomed cottage and in most cases a wooden staging was nailed up beneath the rafters where they could sleep. In time perhaps six or seven offspring might be crowded there under the damp thatch, their bed no more than straw or sacking. As soon as possible these children were found work in the fields or on the mine but for several years the babies remained at home, to fend for themselves if both parents were out working. Many and many a time this unavoidable neglect had dire results, for all too often a child was found dead or injured on their return—drowned, scalded or burned, mauled and bitten by a giant rat perhaps or killed, as in more than one case, by the vicious family pig strayed from its lean-to shed outdoors. Frequently too an unattended child wandered outside to fall beneath the wheels of a passing cart or perhaps down an overgrown mine shaft nearby or into the open cess pit which invariably lay near the door.

Within every cottage the greatest material comfort was always the ever burning fire which was the centre of each humble home. Coal was too costly to buy but there was no shortage of other fuels in the form of brushwood, peat cut from the moors, driftwood from the beaches, or furze. The latter, although regarded as a menace by farmers today, was once sown as seed for cutting, and the gathering of large quantities into a rick was one of the vitally important tasks of the summer months. Piled high in the fireplace built in the great thickness of a cottage wall, furze made a splendid blaze. Over it hung the large iron pot in which broths and stews were cooked. In some cottages a cloam (earthenware) oven was built into the side of the fireplace; otherwise food to be cooked was placed in smaller quantities on to a heated iron plate laid in the hot ashes. It was then covered with an iron dish, that in turn with the glowing embers and the next meal was thus baked to a nicety.

During the whole of their lives, most of the Cornish poor a hundred years ago subsisted principally on pilchards, potatoes, vegetable broths, pasties and similar foods—a diet that was filling rather than sustaining. Those near the coast were familiar with other seafoods, mullet, conger and gurnet for instance, or even limpets in hard times but the pilchard was the fish most readily available to 'the country', who salted thousands down for winter consumption in a variety of soups and pies. No doubt some found their way into the Cornish pasty of barley flour which, although customarily made of 'turmut, tates and mate', could be provided with almost any kind of sweet or savoury filling to suit individual tastes. This was one reason why each pasty was marked with its future consumer's initials on one end—and why he or she started eating at the other, in case a portion was left over for another meal. Traditionally the savoury pasty, compact, satisfying and tasty, was the ideal meal for the miner to take underground and hundreds of thousands must have been eaten in this way far below surface. But the coarse, dark barley flour found its way into the miner's 'mussel bag' in other forms. Great favourites were heavy cake, fuggan and hobbin, in each of which flour and currants played a dominant role, with results as solid, filling and indigestible as their names suggest.

Rarely was the monotony of this heavy diet of the poor relieved except perhaps in farm labourers' cottages where more nutritious foods such as milk or butter made their appearance on the table from time to time, together with beef or mutton on rare occasions. Unmarried farm hands fared even better, sharing both their master's roof and his table, well stocked with dairy produce and with various meats. The miner's or fisherman's family met none of these, the only meat and fat available being that from the family pig, the only drink—apart from contraband liquor and the rare treat of tea—being harvest beer or, failing that, water. The former was brewed from barley in huge copper or iron furnaces, highly dangerous contraptions known now and again to maim somebody by exploding.

On reflection, it must always be a source of wonder that Cornwall's miners and fishermen were able to toil as they did, for long hours and under adverse conditions, on such a diet and with so few creature comforts. For the poor who dwelled in the few towns conditions were no better, however, for they lived in what were described as 'damp, ill ventilated and wretched abodes' with no 'necessaries', and packed around airless courtyards where pigs routed and filth of one sort or another lay ankle deep. Yet they too grafted hard, on the quayside perhaps, as 'scavengers' or refuse gatherers, in stinking tanyard, or among the decaying carcases strewn about the butchers' shambles. Little wonder that the cholera epidemic of the 1830's killed thousands or that small pox, venereal disease, ringworm, tapeworm and hydrophobia were rife, as well as typhus in Scilly. It is to be marvelled at that during this period it was a matter of pride for a man to raise a large family—perhaps twelve or thirteen children—without parochial relief. Such achievements were duly rewarded by public presentation of money prizes, say £2. The proud man, moreover, dreaded the prospect of the workhouse as much as falling on the parish and not because of the conditions there, for if anything they seem from contemporary accounts to have been no worse than those in many a poor home. At least the inmates knew the dubious pleasures of such things as brown cotton sheeting, worsted stockings and hob-nailed boots, yellow soap, iron bedsteads, and mutton and boiling peas.

It was, of course, winter which was most dreaded by the labouring poor, although it was some comfort that this season in Cornwall is usually short and mild. Nevertheless, a very cold spell took its toll of the undernourished and the frail and it was not unknown for the poor to drop dead in the streets in bitter weather. Help was always at hand, although sometimes tardily, from the parish overseers, as well as the county gentry, the latter frequently distributing coal, potatoes, blankets, woollen shirts and the like to those on their estates or sometimes among paupers generally.

The gentry of Cornwall were not notably wealthy and did not include any noblemen of first rank. The principal families, such as the Vyvyans of Trelowarren, the illustrious Grenvilles of Stowe, the Godolphins, Trevelyans, Bassets, Rashleighs, Treffrys, the Trevanions of Caerhays and the staunchly Roman Catholic Arundells of Trerice had been mainly for the defeated King during the Great Civil War a century and a half earlier, and their estates and fortunes had diminished in consequence. Duchy tenants or no, about an equal number of Cornish gentry had supported Parliament, and in the long run, the war cost them dear too, despite generous compensations for their allegiance. Among the Parliamentarians were the Boscawens of Tregothnan (Lord Falmouth's family), the Robartes of Lanhydrock, Eliots of St. Germans, and the St. Aubyns of Clowance, the latter acquiring as reward, for instance, St. Michael's Mount from the Bassets. When later the King was restored to the throne the Royalists were rewarded in turn and many titles as well as offices of importance were distributed amongst them at this time.

Most of these families, landed and titled gentry of no great wealth by national standards, survived to form the nucleus of Cornwall's eighteenth and nineteenth century aristocracy. During this period the fortunate among them recouped some of their wealth as a result of being mineral lords, especially during the great era of Cornish copper production; Lord de Dunstanville, of the Basset family, controlled the great Cook's Kitchen and Dolcoath mines, for instance, while Lord Falmouth owned many rich ones in the parishes of Gwennap and Chacewater. Those who held mineral rights in areas bearing tin or, later, china-clay also were fortunate; these included Lord Falmouth once again, as well as Lord Camelford of Boconnoc—whose forebears joined the Cornish gentry by purchasing the house with the famous Pitt diamond—and the Hawkins of Trewinnard. Some of their numbers thrived also as a result of interests in the promotion of ports and railways to serve the mines; the Bassets, for example, built Portreath, while one of the Treffrys developed Newquay and Par. In addition a number of the 'nouveaux riches' emerged, the new gentry of the nineteenth century, people who rose quickly to pre-eminence as a result of their enterprise—or sometimes their lack of scruples—in the mining field, such as the Lemons of Carclew, near Truro, and the Williams family of Scorrier.

The great families of Cornwall a century ago were not absentee landlords, but largely lived on the estates and, in many cases, in the manor houses of their forebears. Their time was spent largely within their own bounds, concerning themselves with estate management, shooting or fishing perhaps, and reciprocating each other's hospitality with tea-drinking, dining, musical evenings and dancing. Occasionally visits were made to London and the wealthier even wintered abroad. On the whole they were beneficient landlords, showing reasonable interest in their thousands of tenants, farm labourers, tinners, clay workers, long-shoremen and the like, lending a sympathetic ear to pleas for rent reduction in distress, distributing beef or blankets at Christmas, turning a blind eye to the need for eviction on the untimely loss of a last life. They became patrons of the arts and sciences in Cornwall, while their ladies devoted themselves to charities; they disbursed monies for a constant procession of good causes and for several benefactory schemes. The Lemons, for instance, built a part of Truro and endeavoured to establish a mining school there, while the Foxes, a Quaker family of Falmouth, did much to promote the welfare of miners. They also sat on innumerable committees, shared among themselves the more exalted offices such as Sheriff, Lord Lieutenant and Lord Warden of the Stannaries; and sent themselves to Parliament, buying seats at Westminster by scandalous means until the practice was put an end to by the Reform Bill of 1832. In short, until more recent times the affairs and fortunes of the county lay very much in their control.

A number of their manor houses can easily be visited or seen and these enable one to envisage the gap existing between rich and poor in the county a century or so ago. There is Arwenack House in Falmouth, formerly in a beautiful little estate, home of the Killigrews who enriched themselves partly by piracy; Trerice, near Newquay, Elizabethan manor of the Arundells, a family now long departed; St. Michael's Mount; Godolphin Hall; Lanhydrock, near Lostwithiel; Tehidy, now a hospital; and mediaeval Cotehele of the Edgcumbes, in east Cornwall. During the century, which after all was one of prosperity for the rich if not for the poor, several mansions were renovated or rebuilt. Examples are battlemented Tregothnan in its vast estates and deer park, and Treffry's great grey fortress at Fowey. Port Eliot of the Eliots was also reconstructed at this time in the midst of its remarkable landscaped gardens at St. Germans. The parvenus, too, spent their newly acquired wealth in providing themselves with grand houses in equally choice situations, such as the Doric columned Trelissick on the Fal, or the reconstructed Carclew, Caerhays, and Penrose at Helston.

Although the well-to-do visited London to enjoy a cultural and social life not found in Cornwall, the journey was both uncomfortable and protracted. A very few had their own carriages for such an expedition, like the springless Trewinnard coach which has survived the years and is now in the County Museum at Truro. Otherwise it was possible to hire a post-chaise, although a gentleman travelling alone usually found horseback more acceptable over short distances. It was not until the turn of the century that a number of turnpikes were built in Cornwall, the county lagging badly behind the rest of the country as far as ways and means of transport were concerned. Only four existed at this time, all centred on Truro and running thence to Torpoint, Launceston, Falmouth and Penzance. Apart from the latter, these were mainly constructed to carry mails to London from the packet port of Falmouth. All side roads were no more than tracks, in summer rutted and potholed, and in winter an impassable quagmire of puddles and knee-deep in mud. Through these the poor had to struggle when about their daily business, together with the pack animals which were commonly used until the end of the eighteenth century for most transport. Little wonder that the lives of the working poor were closely circumscribed, although there are one or two of their kind on record as having walked to London.

As far as public transport was concerned, various alternatives presented themselves. There were stage-waggons, cumbersome vehicles drawn by teams of strong horses which took about three weeks to reach London. These covered waggons carried all bulky or heavy goods, among which the traveller had to find a seat as well as to spread his coat or blanket on which to sleep at night. The prospect of such a journey, jolted and jarred for days on end, must have been daunting in the extreme and more so when one considers the possibilities of being in close confinement with unsavoury characters. There was no reason why these might not include criminals en route for Launceston gaol, the treadmills at Bodmin or Penzance or the prison hulks at Plymouth.

Better in all these respects were the stage-coaches introduced at the beginning of the nineteenth century. Initially these took about a week to reach the capital but speeds improved under the pressure of competition from the mail-coach service, commenced about the same time. The first of these latter ran from Falmouth over Bodmin Moor to Launceston and Exeter, stopping frequently to change horses. These stages included such celebrated inns as the Norway between Truro and Falmouth, the Indian Queen on Goss Moor, and Jamaica Inn on Bodmin Moor. How many times must children of the labouring poor, perhaps busy in the wintry pools of stream works on Goss Moor, have felt their envious hearts beat faster as the mail-coach thundered by to Roche, blood horses at full gallop, horn echoing to the distant hills, gay livery a streak of colour across their dreary day.

Yet the passengers were not entirely to be envied. Those riding within were cramped and stifled, those on top—at half fare—often soaked to the skin, sometimes unseated and injured, and on one or two occasions even frozen to death. For, on principle, the mail-coaches ran whatever the weather prospect, sometimes to find themselves in the midst of a trackless moor blanketed with snow, the road hidden and known to be flanked on either side by dangerous bogs or ditches. And when at last the welcome inn was reached, the passengers had barely clambered stiffly down before fresh horses were harnessed and the coach ready to be on its way.

Some of these early coaches and post-chaises carried the first intrepid travellers down from London to satisfy their curiosity about the 'barbarous' south-west. Usually the experience proved uncomfortable in the extreme, the accommodation primitive. Nevertheless, certain features of this remote region took them by surprise: Penzance, for instance, unexpectedly fashionable in the early nineteenth century, and home of the country's only Royal Geological Society: the elegant attendance at Truro, Launceston and Bodmin Races in the autumn; and Cornwall's numerous mansions with their surprisingly refined households. But above all it was Truro which caused comment, for by this date the elegant Georgian town was a metropolis of the west, a London in miniature. Many of Cornwall's landed gentry, including the

Lemon, Boscawen, Robartes and Daniell families had town houses there, some of which still stand, their rather austere facades hiding remains of formerly splendid and ornate interiors. There was, for example, the Great House of the Robartes in Boscawen Street and the Daniells' Mansion House in Princes Street, completed in 1762. Prisoners of the French Revolution were responsible for the fashioning of its elaborate ceilings. Adjoining lay Princes House of the Lemon family which today still remains, its fine staircase and ceilings hidden and forgotten. Over a century ago the heart of Truro where these houses lay must have been very picturesque, its wide and cobbled thoroughfares constantly busy with the coming and going of fine carriages and horses, as befitted the county's principal coaching centre and rendezvous of the well-to-do during the winter 'season'. Ladies and gentlemen of fashion attended a constant round of balls, theatre and concerts held usually at the Assembly Rooms, their carriages and sedan chairs during the dark evenings drawing up one after another before its facade of Bath stone embellished with medallions of Garrick and Shakespeare. Meanwhile during the day, young blades could learn the art of fencing in the same building or be taught, along with their sisters and cousins, the minuet, gallopade, cotillion or whatever dance had caught fashion's fancy at the time.

One of the most interesting features of Cornwall in the old days was the diversity of entertainment and sport with which the labouring classes whiled away their hours of leisure. Because they were poor these pastimes inevitably had to be simple and unsophisticated pursuits of the kind which give pleasure in a simple rural community and preferably those in which many could participate, however limited their ability or their purse. Many of these activities took place at certain times of year, being part either of the calendar of those whose daily round was governed largely by the harvesting of their livelihood from sea or land, or else traditional events whose true meaning lay half forgotten and hidden in the mists of time.

Among such regular entertainments were the cellar feasts given by pilchard seine owners for the womenfolk at the end of the season's work, and the harvest suppers provided by farmers for their labourers once the grain was reaped. The quantity of food eaten on these occasions was prodigious, sufficient to nauseate the modern stomach.

Equally incredible were the tremendous amounts of strong beer con-sumed. But gargantuan feasts of this kind seemed customarily to be the accepted kind of celebration for the poor, there being numerous excuses found throughout the year for get-togethers of this kind. There was 'midsummering' for instance and, of course, Christmastide; royal births or accessions were usually celebrated as well as great victories during the Napoleonic wars, as well as the final declaration of peace. Further festivities accompanied the passing of the momentous Reform Bill of 1832, which brought to an end widespread bribery and cor-ruption among the Cornish aristocracy in their bid for parliamentary seats.

On these occasions workers all over the county had the opportunity of sitting down to eat all they could of such fare as roast beef, plum pudding and strong beer—the traditional meal at these times—pro-vided by their masters. Normally such dinners took place out of doors, in town centre, on farm, claywork or mine, with hundreds of people seated at trestle tables stretching perhaps a few score yards. In Liskeard, for instance, there is a record of over 1,500 of the poor sitting down at three hundred yards of tables during the Reform Bill celebrations. The great quantities of food required were cooked in great iron crocks on improvised ovens or roasted whole on a spit over a huge bonfire. After the meal, smaller gatherings often retired to a convenient inn for dancing and drinking, or made their way to the nearest village or town to join in the jollifications there. Major celebrations were normally marked by the elaborate decoration of the better houses by their owners, who were also accustomed to providing quantities of laurel or other evergreens from their estates for the decoration of the streets. No doubt, too, the gentry were responsible for the provision afterwards of firework displays, always enormously popular, as well as illuminations, bell-ringing, processions and bands through the streets and the burning of tar barrels on nearby hillsides.

During the winter months outdoor entertainments were few, with the exception of ploughing and hedging matches, but the summer brought much to keep them amused. There were for instance sheaf-pitching contests, live-stock judging, and the competitions arranged by a number of cottage and rural garden societies, organisations sponsored by the more beneficient landowners to encourage better husbandry. In fact some of the latter actually troubled to introduce new or improved types of vegetables into their tenants' gardens towards this end. Then during the summer various shows were arranged with a view to awarding prizes for several different classes of garden flowers and vegetables as well as pigs, beehives and the like. There was something to be won, too, by the man who had put out most children to trades, and it was on these occasions that he who had reared the largest family on his own earnings was rewarded.

The calendar in Cornwall also featured a large number of fairs which took place on fixed days in various places throughout the length and breadth of the county. One or two of these were innovations of the nineteenth century, like the bi-annual fair at Roche after 1829, but most were of some antiquity, such as Summercourt Fair, a great event attended by vast crowds of people and at which thousands of animals were put up for sale. Other typical gatherings included Lanreath Garland Fair, Bodmin Garland Ox Fair, Mazzard (Cherry) Fair at Tregoney, Helston Gooseberry Fair, a number of Goosey Fairs and the quaintly named Moggy's Fair at Perranwell. These occasions —at least to modern eyes—must have been both spectacular and fascinating, for they brought together a cross-section of the lower classes of Cornish society, including not only the honest and hardworking but also a motley collection of pickpockets, gypsies, fortunetellers, streetwalkers, beggars, vagrants, quack doctors and those who practised charming and witchcraft—two arts slow to vanish from Cornwall.

For the entertainment of the milling and sweating throngs there were always plenty of side shows, amusements and competitions including dancing bears, pole-climbing, jingling, fireworks, bull-baiting, equestrian feats, stilt dancing, pigeon shooting, balloon ascents and the exhibition of human and animal freaks. Tastes no doubt were crude and grew cruder as the liquor flowed and the fair days wore on; drunkenness, indecent conduct, thieving, profane language and even the occasional case of wife-selling were targets for complaint by the more puritan writers to the newspapers of the day.

A lesser and perhaps more respectable assortment of entertainment booths and refreshment stalls usually accompanied other activities such as the various days of 'Annual Diversions' offered by the principal towns, as well as the numerous parish feast days, regattas and annual boat races which were arranged. These latter were normally for working boats, various classes being arranged and they took place offshore in full view of the fishing village concerned. Other regular and exciting races included those for Falmouth quay punts, wherries at Penzance and gigs at St. Ives, while on one occasion at least there was even a lifeboat race, under oars and sail, in Mount's Bay. There were numbers of boat races organised on the Fal each year, and it was usual for the road between Truro and Malpas to be lined with carriages watching those that took place in Truro river. The first prizes for these events were normally silver cups, with silken ensigns and pennants for the runners up. Certainly in those days more pleasure was derived from the water by the people as a whole for, in addition to the regular schooner or paddle steamer services from Cornish ports to London, Plymouth and thence to the Channel Islands or the French coast, there were also many short sea trips available during the summer. These were mainly along the Cornish coast—for instance during the 1830's for 2/6 one could take a scenic offshore excursion from St. Ives north to the Gannel (Newquay) on a boat with a band on board, or southwards round the land to Cape Cornwall.

It is not surprising that a number of the most traditional Cornish pastimes and customs were closely connected with the seasons and the various activities of the farming year. Until quite recently the quaint ceremony of 'crying the neck' was performed on a few Cornish farms; in this, the cutting of the last few stalks of corn was accompanied by an interesting ritual of question and answer among the harvesters present, and the 'neck' or corn was then interwoven with wild flowers and carried to the farmhouse. Here it was put in a place of honour over the kitchen fireplace and, that evening, looked down upon the workers' traditional harvest supper.

Springtime and the return of the sun brought with them other festivities. These included the now famous Furry (meaning 'festival') Day at Helston on May 8th, with its Hal-an-Tow ceremony, and the equally well known May Day celebration at Padstow. The latter includes the weird figure of the Hobbyhorse, a man in a strange black, tent-like cape, a frightening mask, pointed hat and equipped with tail, plume and giant snapping jaws. Throughout the day, teased along by a man in woman's attire, he prances and dances along streets decorated with spring greenery and filled with onlookers, followed by an escort of strangely dressed men who play the tune of the 'Morning Song'. This is a fertility rite of some kind, one in which the horse now and again 'rushes' the women in the crowd. In the last century one man saw fit to try and bribe the onlookers away each year with the promise of an annual gift of a fat bullock, he found the goings-on so unseemly.

The Helston proceedings are rather more decorous, and are best known for the long processions of dancers in fine dresses or top hats and tails, who make their way along the streets, in and out of the houses and shops. But the Hal-an-Tow which precedes this is the oldest and most significant part of the day's events. In this pagan rite, no longer properly observed, the return of summer was welcomed by the playing of the compelling 'Day Song', while branches of May (sycamore) were brought into the town early in the morning from the surrounding countryside.

In a further ceremony to mark the summer solstice, another originally pagan festival was celebrated throughout Cornwall, bonfires being lit on the higher hills from Kit Hill westwards at midnight on June 23rd. No doubt the accompanying jollifications, such as dancing, singing and drinking, as well as the carrying of torches and lighting of tar barrels, which continued long into the small hours of the warm summer night, were a relic of pre- Christian days when man revered the sun and welcomed its return after the dead, dark days of the long winter.

Different again was the ancient sport of hurling. This rough and tumble game still takes place at St. Columb and St. Ives but in former days it was more widespread and even more boisterous. There were several variations on the game but all seemed to have involved few rules and few restrictions on the number of participants, which meant every able bodied man joined in with gusto. Cuts, bruises and the occasional broken bone were the accepted order of the day as the two teams of menfolk struggled for possession of the hurling ball to carry it 'to goal'—a distance of possibly four or five miles—or perhaps out of the parish. The ball was of applewood encased in silver, a symbol so it is said of the sun as it climbs the sky towards the summer solstice. An early account of hurling indicates that the most successful team was probably that which included a number of good wrestlers. This latter is the one which above all epitomises the Cornishman in the field of sport, although during the nineteenth century it gradually declined. There was a time when open air wrestling matches were attended by thousands and were held over a period of several days. During such a match the number of contestants was gradually whittled down to give one single winner, unless it was a grand contest between two wrestlers of great note, such as the famous Polkinghorne of Cornwall and Cann of Devon, who fought in the 1820's. The style of wrestling in these two counties differed, for in Devonshire nailed wrestling shoes and leg pads were worn while the Cornish normally fought in stockinged feet; consequently whenever a match was arranged between them alternate bouts were fought in each style. Sometimes the winners were awarded purses of sovereigns; for instance in a match at Penzance in 1828, these constituted the first five prizes, the sixth a gold-laced hat and the seventh one laced with silver. It is interesting that similar unusual prizes— gold-laced hats, white hats, silver-laced hat bands and so on, were the normal prizes carried off in that other favourite—more gentle—Cornish pastime, a bell-ringing contest between parishes.

Most of these festive public occasions—as well as the remarkable walking funerals of the day, where hundreds singing hymns followed the chief mourners on foot—were excuses for drinking on a large scale. Even in the poorest home there was usually a supply of cheap liquor, either come ashore with the last wreck in the locality or bought for next to nothing from the 'moonshine brigade', who organised constant supplies from the coast of France. In addition no man—or woman— had far to walk to the nearest public house, kiddleywink, brandy or gin shop, and often enough the innkeeper added further inducement by arranging a succession of entertainments such as wrestling bouts, cock-fights or similar, on his premises. Little wonder that practically every public gathering in Cornwall one or two hundred years ago was accompanied by riotousness and violence in one form or another.

It was against this background of such wickednesses as smuggling, wrecking, piracy and drunkenness that John Wesley preached when he first visited Cornwall in 1743, although he disapproved strongly of the more innocuous wrestling and hurling too. His audiences usually comprised violent and hard drinking tinners, yet for all that the Cornish were an instinctively religious people affording fertile ground for the seeds Wesley was to sow. Despite much opposition, including even violence, Wesley and his followers persisted in preaching long and often throughout the mining districts for many successive years. Eventually they overcame the prejudices and dislikes they met with, instilling in their followers the discipline of an austere religion. As a result, there gradually sprang up hundreds of Methodist chapels throughout

Victorian Cornwall

Cornwall, which by 1840 was a stronghold of this new sect. These chapels, it may be added, were often built in similar fashion to the cottages of the labouring poor, by their communal effort after a long day's work. There were also Sunday schools by the early nineteenth century, some inter-denominational, which taught not only religion but the three R's, and which preceded the day schools. By and by the Sunday school annual treat became one of the major events in each locality and might be attended by as many as four hundred children or more. Frequently it took the form of an excursion to the sea, either by waggon or by train, and sometimes meant a visit to the mansion of the nearby landowner, where decorous games might be enjoyed on the lawns.

By the mid nineteenth century Wesleyanism in Cornwall was at its height and its sobering effects over the years, together with the increasing strength of the law, had put an end to smuggling, wrecking, drunkenness and such brutalities as bull-baiting and cock fighting. The second half of the century saw further changes which led towards the same end. The network of better communication after the main line railway system of Britain reached into Cornwall in the 1860's became increasingly used by a new breed of traveller—the holidaymaker. And their seasonal invasion of Cornwall was to become the saviour of the county's economy, after the mining era came to a close and that other great staple, the fishing industry, had all but died. But while it saved Cornwall's economic fate it began at the same time the slow, inexorable destruction of all the things truly Cornish which marked it out as a land apart from the rest of these islands.